Dear artists,

May each brushstroke within these pages be an expression of your inner world, a reflection of the vibrant hues of your dreams, and the landscapes of your imagination. May this book not just be a coloring space, but a magical portal that ignites your creativity, allowing you to dive into an ocean of possibilities.

May every stroke be a celebration of your uniqueness, for each artwork is a journey in itself, an opportunity to discover new ways of seeing and interpreting the world around you.

With love and admiration for your infinite palettes of colors.

Daniella Vasconcelos

2024

This Book Belongs to:

Test Color Page

www.ingramcontent.com/pod-product-compliance
Lightning Source LLC
Chambersburg PA
CBHW080937260726
48661CB00010B/3954